Imagems 2

By Richard Berengarten

SELECTED WRITINGS: SHEARSMAN EDITION

Vol. 1   *For the Living : Selected Longer Poems, 1965–2000*
Vol. 2   *The Manager*
Vol. 3   *The Blue Butterfly* (Part 1, *The Balkan Trilogy*)
Vol. 4   *In a Time of Drought* (Part 2, *The Balkan Trilogy*)
Vol. 5   *Under Balkan Light* (Part 3, *The Balkan Trilogy*)
Vol. 6   *Manual: the first hundred*
Vol. 7   *Notness: Metaphysical Sonnets*
Vol. 8   *Changing*
Vol. 9   *A Portrait in Inter-Views*

OTHER POETRY

Avebury
The Easter Rising 1967
The Return of Lazarus
Double Flute
Inhabitable Space
Some Poems, Illuminated by Frances Richards
Learning to Talk
Roots/Routes
Half of Nowhere
Against Perfection
Book With No Back Cover
Do vidjenja Danice (Goodbye Balkan Belle)

AS EDITOR

An Octave for Octavio Paz
Ceri Richards: Drawings to Poems by Dylan Thomas
Rivers of Life
In Visible Ink: Selected Poems, Roberto Sanesi, 1955–1979
Homage to Mandelstam
Out of Yugoslavia
For Angus
The Perfect Order: Selected Poems, Nasos Vayenas, 1974–2010
IDEA and ACT

PROSE

Keys to Transformation: Ceri Richards and Dylan Thomas
Imagems (1)

Imagems 2

Richard Berengarten

Shearsman Books

First published in the United Kingdom in 2019 by
Shearsman Books
50 Westons Hill Drive
Emersons Green
BRISTOL
BS16 7DF

Shearsman Books Ltd Registered Office
30–31 St. James Place, Mangotsfield, Bristol BS16 9JB
(this address not for correspondence)

www.shearsman.com

ISBN 978-1-84861-685-1

ACKNOWLEDGEMENTS

Thanks to the editors of the following for publishing earlier versions of
these texts: *International Literary Quarterly* ('English Writers 2', December
2015, online) for 'On Poetry and Sound: the Ontogenesis of Poetry'
and 'On Writing and Inner Speech'; *Whirlwinds of Words Across the
Daliangshan Highlands, Anthology of Poems and Essays* (Xichang-Qionghai
Silk Road International Poetry Week, June 2016) for 'On Universalism
and Particularism'; and *Margutte* (posted online, June 2019), for 'On
Universalism and Particularism', 'On the Breath and the Cry', 'On Poetry
and Exile' and 'On Poetry and Morning'. My special thanks, too, to my
wife, Melanie Rein and to Paul S. Derrick for their invaluable suggestions
on several near-final drafts. The cover shows a sketch of the author by Marin
Sorescu in Belgrade, 1982.

Contents

Not Chaos, not
The darkest pit of lowest Erebus,
Nor aught of blinder vacancy, scooped out
By help of dreams, can breed such fear and awe
As fall upon us often when we look
Into our Minds, into the Mind of Man,
My haunt, and the main region of my Song …
WILLIAM WORDSWORTH

[*I*]*n its own terms* there is no way that language can break out of the world language creates – except by allowing language to go beyond itself in poetry…
IAIN MCGILCHRST

There is nothing that cannot be said and it is possible to say nothing.
PIERRE BOURDIEU

On Poetry and Sound:
The Ontogenesis of Poetry

Twelve Propositions

1. Where and how does poetry begin in a person's world? I contend, first, that its origins are in rhythm and, more specifically, sound rhythms; and second, that these sounds are pre-linguistic. They occur in the womb of the mother, before the ears of the foetus have fully developed as organs and well before full aural exposure to language as a referential system can possibly have occurred. In short, the ontological origins of both poetry and music precede birth. They are intra-uterine.

2. Rhythm itself means habit and familiarity. What constitutes rhythm of any kind is, precisely, the patterning of regularity, repetition, ritual. These features and functions overlap, merge and cohere. Familiarity is primary. Rhythm is familiar because it belongs and pertains to the family and arises from the first familial condition: that of the foetus in the womb. Being by definition regular and repetitive, sound rhythm develops a sense of *safety, security* and *surety* for the foetus. Rhythm, which means *wave motion*, confirms, comforts, consoles and conditions.

3. The developing human foetus is bombarded constantly by multiple sounds from its environment, the all-encompassing body of the mother. First, there are the noises that come from the interior of the mother's body. These include the intermittent peristaltic whisperings, gurglings and swooshings of the mother's digestive process. Even more regularly, the foetus registers the secure background rhythms of the mother's breathing, and the pitter-patter of her heart as it pumps and pulses blood. Here is the beginning of every human being's sense of music. We might call it a proto-music. In a study as detailed and delicate as it is profound and far-reaching, Giselle E. Whitwell collates and synthesises recent research by foetologists as follows:

Uterine sounds form a "sound carpet" over which the mother's voice in particular appears very distinct and which the prenate gives special attention to because it is so different from its own amniotic environment. These sounds are of major importance because they establish the first patterns of communication and bonding. Some researchers have discovered that newborns become calmer and more self-regulated when exposed to intrauterine sound [...]. The soothing sounds of the ocean and water are probably reminiscent of the fluid environment in which we began life. Tomatis suggests that the maternal heart beat, respiration and intestinal gurgling, all form the source for our collective attraction to the sound of surf and may have to do with our inborn sense of rhythm. Prenatal sounds form an important developmental component in prenatal life because they provide a foundation for later learning and behavior. (Whitwell 1999)

4.   The foetus also registers sounds that come from outside the mother. The mother listens to music, she drives in traffic, a dog barks, other humans make sounds in her presence, including speech sounds. The foetus's senses cannot be entirely blockaded by the mother's protective body, and all of these affect the foetus, in ways not yet fully understood, even if they are muffled and filtered by the various layered organs and membranes of the mother's body. "Many pregnant women report a fetal jerk or sudden kick just after a door slams or a car backfires," writes Janet Hopson (1998).

5.   Evidently, then, the foetus/embryo is exposed to sound rhythms at all stages of development; and perception and registration of sound begin very early. The embryo begins to develop a cerebral cortex after only five weeks. "At nine weeks, the embryo's ballooning brain allows it to bend its body, hiccup, and react to loud sounds" (ibid.). By 17 weeks, the vocal chords have formed (SPUC, 'Foetal Development'). Furthermore:

Estimates of the date at which the human foetus begins to hear currently range between 16 and 24 weeks gestational age (GA), depending, *inter alia*, upon the kind of sound presented and the exact criterion according to which hearing is deemed to be present. At 20 weeks GA, the human cochlea reaches a developmental state similar to that in other mammals when responses to sound can be evoked, and sounds may be encoded and messages sent along the auditory pathways.

Abundant anecdotal evidence exists regarding the effect of sound heard prenatally upon the behaviour of the new-born infant. For example, in 6th century Europe, it was believed that sounds, conversations and especially music heard by the unborn child affected the personality and disposition of the baby after birth. (IIP Services)

"By the end of the second trimester, it can hear" (Hopson). "A very premature baby entering the world at 24 or 25 weeks responds to the sounds around it [...], so its auditory apparatus must already have been functioning in the womb" (ibid.). Whitwell observes:

> The ear first appears in the 3rd week of gestation and it becomes functional by the 16th week. The fetus begins active listening by the 24th week. We know from ultrasound observations that the fetus hears and responds to a sound pulse starting about 16 weeks of age [...]; *this is even before the ear construction is complete.* The cochlear structures of the ear appear to function by the 20th week and mature synapses have been found between the 24th and 28th weeks. [. . .] *The sense of hearing is probably the most developed of all the senses before birth.* (Whitwell, 'The Sound environment of the Womb'; emphases added)

Some researchers suggest that the mother's body is no barrier at all to the foetus's developing hearing:

> Until recently, it was thought that the sound of the mother's voice was masked by the strong sounds of her heartbeat and other internal organs. However, it is now well established that external speech sounds, including the mother's voice, can be heard clearly inside the womb. (Harris and Butterworth 143)

We may also infer that the partial permeability of the mother's body to sound, especially voice, serves as a conditioning, preparatory or educative purpose in the foetus's pre-linguistic development.

6. As a distinct sub-category of sound, the foetus also registers the mother's own oral sounds, as she talks, hums, sings, murmurs, snores, shouts, laughs, etc. And although the general observation made in the last quoted observation by Harris and Butterworth is likely to be accurate as far as it goes, it needs to be emphasised that, from the foetus's perspective, acoustically the mother's voice is not merely "external". For her speech sounds begin in her vocal chords and vibrate to the foetus through the membranes of organs in the interior of her body as well as from the projection of the sounds onto surrounding air. Since the mother's voice resonates to the foetus from *both* inside *and* outside her body, we may also infer that the foetus experiences the mother's voice not merely as intimate but as all-pervasive.

7. Apart from sign languages used by the deaf and dumb, primary language transmission occurs by sound: it is universally vocal and its reception universally oral. So here are the beginnings of a human being's sense of language. And even though, obviously, the referentiality of language to specific objects in the exterior world cannot begin to be fully recognised and determined until well after birth, according to Hopson the work by De Casper and colleagues at the University of North Carolina suggests that a foetus: (a) can distinguish between individual voices; (b) prefers the voice of its mother to those of others, "especially the way it sounds filtered through amniotic fluid rather than through air"; and (c) also prefers to hear the rhythms of the mother "speaking in her native language than to hear her or someone else speaking in a foreign tongue" (Hopson). The same author reports that Lecanuet and colleagues in Paris have found that foetuses (a) distinguish between strangers' voices, and (b) prefer certain stories to others:

> The fetal heartbeat will slow down when a familiar French fairy tale such as 'La Poulette' ('The Chick') or 'Le Petit Crapaud' ('The Little Toad'), is read near the mother's belly. When the same reader delivers another unfamiliar story, the fetal heartbeat stays steady. [...] The fetus is likely responding to the *cadence of voices and stories, not their actual words*, observes Fifer, but the conclusion is the same:

the fetus can listen, learn, and remember at some level, and, as with most babies and children, *it likes the comfort and reassurance of the familiar'* (ibid.; emphases added).

8. Some researches on the perception of language rhythms by the foetus are as astonishing in their correspondence to expectation and intuition as they are beautiful. Here is Whitwell again:

> Verny and others have noted that babies have a preference for stories, rhymes, and poems first heard in the womb. When the mother reads out loud, the sound is received by her baby in part via bone conduction. Dr. Henry Truby, Emeritus Professor of Pediatrics and Linguistics at the University of Miami, points out that after the sixth month, the fetus moves in rhythm to the mother's speech and that spectrographs of the first cry of an abortus at 28 weeks could be matched with his mother's. *The elements of music, namely tonal pitch, timbre, intensity and rhythm, are also elements used in speaking a language.* For this reason, music prepares the ear, body and brain to listen to, integrate and produce language sounds. *Music can thus be considered a pre-linguistic language* which is nourishing and stimulating to the whole human being, affecting body, emotions, intellect, and developing an internal sense of beauty, sustaining and awakening the qualities in us that are wordless and otherwise inexpressible (Whitwell: 'Introduction'; emphases added).

9. All of these observations support the theory that, ontologically, sound is chronologically far more significant than vision in the very earliest formation of both language and poetry. Just as the rhythmical sounds experienced by the foetus constitute a proto-music, so the speech-sounds experienced constitute a proto-language and a proto-poetry.

10. If these contentions are accepted, and if language is considered as a referential and representational system whose primary function, individually and communally, is to register, co-ordinate and regulate spatial and temporal relationships and phenomena, then it might be said: that proto-poetic rhythms are patterned into the body before anything like an 'image' even gets a look in.

11. Or, if the meaning of the word *image* is to be extended beyond its usual reliance on the visual (eidetic) sense, then sound-rhythms are among the first 'imagings' ('imaginings') to be formulated by the foetus's brain. I have coined the noun, *imagem*, to mean "a unit of interior consciousness expressed in a word, relating to the verbalisation of any sense impression". (For further meanings see also p. 30 below and RB 2013: 26).

12. The foetus, then, is the recipient of a proto-music (from a wide variety of rhythmical sounds, internal and external to the mother), and of a proto-poetry or proto-song (from a wide variety of vocal sounds, which again are both internal and external). The transmission of sounds itself confirms and supports the uniquely intimate bonding between mother and foetus.. Even before the birth of expressive and referential language, musical and poetic rhythms pulse and reverberate in the foetus's blood, bones and brain, filtered through the mother's body.

REFERENCES

Berengarten, Richard. 2013. *Imagems 1*. Bristol: Shearsman Books.

Boeree, C. George. 2003. 'Prenatal development'. Online at: http://webspace.ship.edu/cgboer/genpsyfetaldev.html

Harris, Margaret, and Butterworth, George. 2001. *Developmental Psychology, A Student's Handbook*. London and New York: Psychology Press. Online at: https://books.google.co.uk/

Hopson, Janet L. 1998 (October). 'Fetal Psychology' in *Psychology Today*. Online at: http://www.leaderu.com/orgs/tul/psychtoday9809.htm

IIP Services. (WO/2001/049176) 'Method and Device for Determining and/or Treating Congenital Deafness'. Consulted, January 21-22, 2009. No longer available online.

SPUC, The Society for the Protection of Unborn Children. 2002. 'Foetal Development'. Consulted, January 21-22, 2009. No longer available online.

Whitwell, Giselle. E. 1999. 'The Importance of Prenatal Sound and Music'. *Journal of Prenatal & Perinatal Psychology & Health*, 13: 3-4. Online at: https://www.questia.com/library/journal/1P3-1380679911/the importance-of-prenatal-sound-and-music

On the Breath and the Cry

Twelve Propositions

1. In the beginning was the breath. Then came the cry.

2. When the newborn baby first meets air (greets the world), the midwife makes sure the baby cries. Like all other later cries, that first cry is borne on an outbreath.

3. In order to have the strength to cry, the baby must have lungs full of air. The reason the midwife gets the baby to cry is to make sure that the baby has already drawn breath. A healthy cry means healthy inbreath and outbreath. That cry is evidence (sign, signal) of prior breath. Breath (is what) has priority.

4. Once out of the mother's guardian body, that involuntary taking (sucking) in of air is the first independent nourishment the baby gets (receives) from the world. Inbreath is needed (drawn in, got, received, taken), so that (and so long as) the baby is to live (to be). Breath is the world's first birth-gift and air is the baby's birthright. Before milk.

5. That cry is a call (to) and a claim on the whole world. On and to the whole of mothering and fathering creation.

6. That first human cry is the universal prototype of all speech sounds and archetype of speech in all languages. The first vowel. The first syllable.

7. What the cry says is *Am*. What it utters is *Here Now*. What it voices is *World*. What it calls is *Greeting*. What it announces is *Being*. What it predicts is *Life, Death*. What fills it is *Spirit*.

8. That cry is the governor and founder of all language and ground of all poems and songs. It is the proto-word that contains (holds within it) and foretells (predicts, prophesies, presages) all linguistic forms (shapes, figures) – from phonemes to syllables, from 'parts of speech' to entire grammars.

9. And that cry is bounded by nothing but breath (inbreath). It hangs on breath. Built on breath, made on breath, standing on breath, it's bounded (limited, contained, constrained) by nothing but breath.

10. The length, rhythm, strength, pitch and stress of that first cry cast out into, through and across space-time are the living formants of poetic necessity. Its wave form is the first pattern for the poetic line. It is predecessor alike of the elegant phrase and the abrupt exclamation, the modulated and articulate paragraph and the polite request or snappy command, the curse and blessing, statement and question, speech and paragraph, plea and prayer.

11. Breath is what happens to air through creatures in lived space-time. That is: breath is the wave-form-and-motion taken by air moving in and out of the living animal, as (while, so long as) that creature lives and moves.

12. First comes the Breath and then the Cry. That cry, this cry. Long before the Word.

On Writing and Inner Speech

Twelve Propositions

1. Writing or script, including printing, engraving and typing, may be thought of as one of several possible actualisations of what Lev Vygotsky calls "inner speech",* which, rather than being expressed through the mouth and uttered by the voice, has been interrupted and diverted, to be articulated by the hand or hands.* (Asterisks indicate endnotes: see 30-33 below.)

2. Inner speech doesn't necessarily result in action or activity of any kind, whether linguistic or non-linguistic. Much, perhaps most of it, may get dissipated or lost before it ever reaches any such stage – dissolving, as it were, back into its matrix, whatever that might be, evaporating into thin air. Osip Mandelstam tapped deep into this mysterious process in his lines: "I've forgotten what I wanted to say, / and a bodiless thought sinks back into the world of shadows" (see Mandelstam 1973: 52, and 1987: 90-91; modified tr.). Mandelstam's verb *say* could easily be replaced by *do*.*

3. "Inner speech is a paradoxical phenomenon. It is an experience that is central to many people's everyday lives, and yet it presents considerable challenges to any effort to study it scientifically" (Alderson-Day and Fernyhough). Because it isn't directly observable, inner speech is elusive to the point of being impossible to separate from its background. Scans of brain rhythms, for example, have so far produced no definitive simultaneous correlations with inner speech. For such reasons, inner speech can only be tracked with any degree of confidence *once it has already been externalised* (uttered, manifested): that is, when by definition it's no longer 'inner' at all. Therefore, any such tracking must inevitably be retrospective, introspective and tentatively inferential. Even so, once one's own inner speech *has* been externalised, one may be able to recognise – or at least intuit – that it has consisted of various degrees and modes of processing and patterning,

from the fleetingly spontaneous, momentarily liminal and hintingly approximate, to the partially or well formulated and the consciously purposive (goal-oriented, teleonomic).

4. Before or during its actualisation, inner speech is likely to have been modified and revised iteratively. In particular, inner speech that has been articulated and transformed into (and by) writing tends to be patterned more deliberatively than when it has been converted into oral expression. What's more, the spoor of inner speech may be easier to track via writing than via speech, for at least three separate though inter-related reasons. First, writing is both a visual and a relatively fixed medium. As such, its markings necessarily involve spatial registration on a surface of some kind, so that it affords at least some degree of durability through time. Hence the continuous availability for repeated consultation. Third, the act or process of writing involves the act or acts of composition, i.e. (usually) more conscious attention and effort than speaking. And fourth, a writer is likely to find that, experientially, inner speech is almost 'hearable' between the bursts of manual activity that constitute writing itself. All this suggests that, approached retrospectively from the episodic events of script-production, inner speech may well be inferred to have served a variety of preliminary or preparatory functions, both primary and intermediate. These include: the stirring and loosening of latent (subliminal) material, as well as its sifting, selecting and sorting, in, through and from the memory-reservoir (image-bank, thought-vault, etc.), some of whose contents may get activated as far as the various stages of externalisation. The first linguistic actualisations or articulations of inner speech in writing may take the form of, for example, a private note or notes, a diary entry, a shopping list, a personal memorandum or 'to do' list, a set of 'rough' jottings for a lecture or speech, a draft for a poem, etc.

5. Such writing is partly and perhaps even entirely "egocentric" in Piaget's precise sense (Piaget 1945: 45; Piaget 1969: 208; Vygotsky, 16ff), since in all these cases the writer is either the sole or the prime intended reader. And such notes are likely to be relatively cryptic, disorderly, idiosyncratic, and hurried. They're private, in the sense

of not necessarily being easily comprehensible to anybody else but the writer-as-reader, whether for reasons of form, such as the lack of transparency of scribbled handwriting, their illegibility to others, etc.; or of content, such as obscurity or ambiguity, the lack of knowledge by others of the context of the writing, or the writer's actual or intended meaning or meanings, plus the use of shorthand, code, disguise or idiosyncratic referencing mode, etc. (When returning to lightning-speed jottings I've made for myself, sometimes even *I-as-reader* fail fully to decipher my own scrawled handwriting, or to remember its original context or my original intention. In the interval between writing and reading, whoever scribbled those notes has become no longer 'I' but 'someone else'.) What's more, even if a piece of writing is intended primarily as a message for another or others, its writer always has the chance to read (check) it first, and indeed may wish or prefer to do so. So the writer is by implication always included among those 'others', i.e. as a potential reader. And the writer as self-reader becomes at least partially other, in the act of a reading that is a re-reading.

6. Consecutive preliminary drafts of a poem may therefore mark (track, trace, map, record) various stages in the conversion (transmutation, translation) of inner speech to external articulation: from scarcely verbalised hints and inklings to intricately patterned composition. Comparative examination of such texts can be profoundly insightful: see, for example Jon Stallworthy's study of W. B. Yeats' drafts, suitably entitled *Between the Lines*. Similarly, study of variant versions and revisions of a text are equally likely to enable the mapping of stages in the workings of an author's inner speech: for example comparison between the 1805 and 1850 editions of *The Prelude*. Long before twentieth century linguists and psychologists paid attention to the connections between language and thought, poets were exploring, tapping and articulating these inner processes. This interiorising tendency has been increasingly manifest in the last two centuries, as the first epigraph to this book from Wordsworth suggests. Among novelists, Proust and Joyce *require* their readers to think about language and inner speech to such an extent that the intricacies of this inner relationship might well be inferred to have been the prime focus of their attention.

7. Throughout human history, the variety of material and immaterial surfaces deployed to receive and register writing (including printing, typing and engraving) is enormous: clay, shell, animal bone, turtle plastron and carapace, glass, stone, metal (from bronze and lead to aluminium and other modern metals), silk and all types of woven and knitted fabric, leather, fur, live skin (in branding and tattooing), wood (especially bamboo), wax, paper, plastics, and photographic, filmic, digital and virtual media – have all been deployed (Tsien 2013). What's more, very ancient writing technologies continue to be used alongside new ones that are continually being invented and applied in the now (Edgerton 2006). Until very recently, the production of writing necessarily involved initial activation by hand or hands. Tools for writing include stylus, chisel, chalk, wax, brush, a vast variety of pens (fountain pen, ballpoint, rollerball, felt tip, highlighter, gel pen), pencil, crayon, and many machines involving printing, including fax, photocopier and dot-printer (for braille), typewriter and keyboard combined with digital printer. And now we also have machines capable of producing writing by means of voice recognition and even eye recognition. In all cases, whatever the surface, the result is *text*, every copy of which is capable of functioning as a new original for further replication and dissemination. Signs breed signs. Writing, the sign of a sign of a sign, the sign of signs, breeds writing. Writings breed writings.

8. It follows that a *prerequisite* for a written text to exist may well be that its author's inner speech be purposively directed towards its making. This tallies perfectly with Vygotsky's idea that "besides its role of accompaniment to activity and its expressive and release functions, egocentric speech readily assumes *a planning function*, i.e. turns into *thought proper* quite naturally and easily" (Vygotsky 2012: 92-92; emphasis added). Is the day coming when our machines will have evolved to the point at which we'll be able to transform planned and directed inner speech (i.e. "thought proper") into writing *with no bodily mediation or intervention other than mental concentration and focus*?

9.	However, not only individual words but variations on words, word-combinations and word-patterns also occur in dreams, day-dreams, random musings, and all forms of non-directed thought. They range in intelligibility from glossolalia, babble, wholly or partially incomprehensible utterances, and actual or imagined 'foreign' ('glagolitic') speech, to occurrences and manifestations of language that are meaningfully articulated and entirely intelligible to the person experiencing them. They may occur as 'heard voices' of persons or figures, known or unknown, or they may appear not to belong to any particular voice. They may be experienced as possessing the power and authority of epiphanic revelations from divine entities, spirits and ghosts, whether benevolent or otherwise. All of these phenomena, across their whole range, surely need to be classified as inner speech. What's more, when we experience inner speech, we may experience ourselves as speakers, as listeners, or as both simultaneously. *The singular other is inside myself, as are all plural others.* And while such utterances, together with their hearings, overhearings and underhearings, clearly belong to inner speech, it would equally clearly be difficult to argue that they *all* have a *purposive* function in any purely, simply or even predominantly directional or utilitarian sense. But they may have a *heuristic* function: a person who experiences inner speech in this way may 'get an idea' and so be or feel motivated, directed and even propelled towards action of some sort. Furthermore, many experiments have been made in transmitting (transforming, translating) inner speech to writing without conscious volition or intention, for example by suggestion, including hypnosis, and through automatic writing.

10.	A practised and experienced writer gradually learns to 'listen out', or rather, 'listen in' for inner speech of this kind and to jot it down for possible later use as soon as it surfaces. A poet, for example, may sometimes 'receive' a word-combination and even a rhythmically composed phrase or line or stanza in this way. The Muses of Ancient Greece, the inspirational daughters of Mnemosyne, are as much bearers of inner speech as the angelic calls that beckoned St. Joan, or the voice of Yahweh or his *Shekhinah* ('Presence') that

Moses heard outside his tent. For a poet, hearing or receiving inner speech – initially, as it were, passively rather than actively – may well be identical with the first incipient stirring of verbal impression in his/her mind, even when such an iteration is unexpected and far from being the result of focused or directed attention. Evidently, if not lost in the "world of shadows", and if gathered and remembered, this impression may later be expressed: i.e. may be transformed, developed and registered as a piece of writing. What's more, although for millennia a written text was the only way of recording (fixing, freezing, preserving) speech utterances, since the mid-nineteenth century, we've possessed technologies that directly record sounds, including voiced speech (Berengarten and Dillon 151ff); and we now have machines that convert script to sound and vice-versa.

11. As a precondition for their existence, then, both visual text and speech recordings require inner speech, whether such speech is sensed as the outcome of vague intention or a deliberate plan to compose, or of partly or wholly unexpected inspiration, visitation or revelation. In the latter situations, inner speech is often itself experienced, or at least later processed and retrospectively described, in such terms as a gift, a dictation, a visit, a visitation from afar, a welling up from depths, a descent from on high, and so on. What's more, inner speech may also appear or later be interpreted as an imprinting, or other form of 'marking', and therefore, may intrinsically posit either some kind of *originary act of writing* or cloudy synaesthetic mental conflation of the faculties of hearing and sight. The Kabbalistic text, *Sefer ha-Bahir* [*Book of Illumination*] reports: "All the people *saw the voices*" (Wolfson: 347; emphasis added). Based on how and what Vygotsky wrote of inner speech, can we then be justified in speaking of "inner writing" too? At any rate, all these characterisations of inner speech imply the *otherness* and mysteriousness of its source or sources; and all are loaded either with varying degrees of respect, awe, wonder, and even epiphany and numinosity, or with a sense of irritation, interruption, unwarranted intrusion, and even of temptation, fear, and danger. What's more, inner speech may sometimes take

the form of an inner dialogue, of interplay between two or more interior voices, and even of interior drama. These factors, all of which relate to processes in dream and daydream, apply as clearly to the inner speech that informs the writing of a mature person as they do to the babble of an infant in the crib (Weir 1962).

12. The identities of the voices that utter inner speech haven't yet been adequately accounted for theoretically, whether behaviourally, psychologically or metaphysically; and perhaps they never will be. Meanwhile, Baudelaire's *hypocrite lecteur* remains not just a "semblable" or "frère", but may well be the writer himself/herself. And Rimbaud's remark, "Je est un autre," may be reconfigured as "*L'autre que je suis est toi*" (Burns 2002).

REFERENCES

Alderson-Day, Ben and Fernyhough, Charles. 2015 Sept. 'Inner Speech: Development, Cognitive Functions, Phenomenology, and Neuro-biology'. *Psychological Bulletin*. American Psychological Association. 141(5): 931–965. Online at: https://www.ncbi.nlm.nih.gov/pmc/articles/PMC4538954/

Bahir, The. 1979. Aryeh Kaplan (tr.). York Beach, Maine: Samuel Weiser.

Baudelaire, Charles. 1968. 'Au lecteur' and 'Le voyage', in *Fleurs du mal*. Crépet, Jacques and Blin, Georges (eds.). Paris: Librairie José Corti.

Berengarten, Richard and Dillon, John Z. 2017. 'The Interview as Text and Performance'. In Nikolaou, P. and Dillon, J. Z. (eds.) *A Portrait in Inter-Views*. Bristol: Shearsman Books: 147-174.

Burns, Richard (*aka* Berengarten). 2002 (May 13). 'Pour Toi', Address to the Conference, *Une poétique mondiale de la poésie?* Paris: La Bibliothèque nationale de France.

Edgerton, David. 2006. *The Shock of the Old: Technology and Global History since 1900*. London: Profile.

Mandelstam, Osip. 1973. *Selected Poems*. Brown, Clarence and Merwin, W. S. (trs.). Harmondsworth: Penguin Books.

———. 1987. *Tristia*. McClelland, Bruce (tr.). Barrytown, NY: Station Hill Press.

Piaget, Jean. 1959. *The Language and Thought of the Child*. London: Routledge and Kegan Paul.

———. 1969. *Language and Reasoning in the Child*. London: Rout-ledge and Kegan Paul.

Rimbaud, Arthur. 1966 *Complete Works, Selected Letters* (bilingual French-English edn.). Fowlie, Wallace (tr. and ed.). Chicago, IL: University of Chicago Press.

Stallworthy, Jon. 1963. *Between the Lines: W.B. Yeats's Poetry in the Making*. Oxford: Oxford University Press.

Tsien, Tsuen-Hsuin. 2013 [1962]. *Written on Bamboo and Silk: The Beginnings of Chinese Books and Inscriptions*. Chicago, IL and London: University of Chicago Press.

Vygotsky, Lev. 2012 [1962]. *Thought and Language*. Hanfmann, Eugenia and Walker, Gertrude (trs.); Kozulin, Alex (ed.). Cambridge, MA: MIT Press.

Weir, Ruth Hirsch. 1962. *Language in the Crib*. The Hague: Mouton.

Wolfson, Elliot R. 1994. *Through a Speculum That Shines: Vision and Imagination in Medieval Jewish Mysticism*. Princeton, NJ: Princeton University Press.

Wordsworth, William. *The Prelude:* 1805 and 1850 edns. Online at http://triggs.djvu.org/djvu-editions.com/WORDSWORTH/Testframes.html

On Universalism and Particularism
or

Looking at Flowers Again

Twelve Propositions

1. For poets, as for everyone else, the challenges, dangers, possibilities and hopes of our epoch are enormous. Our time is unlike any other. We have lived through modernism: we know all about that. And we have gone through, or past, post-modernism – even if many of us still don't quite know what that was, or even if it was really anything at all. Modernism is dead. Postmodernism was stillborn. We know this. We sense it in our guts and our bones. They were both pretty silly labels anyway, too self-contradictory to be interesting, and eventually, too overloaded to mean much, if anything at all.

2. As for our own epoch, as yet it has no name, no convenient label. Perhaps, rightly, we've come to suspect all labels. For many of us have grown as wary of the dangers of own irony towards labels as we have always been of the labels themselves. So perhaps a label is the last thing we need. Even so, under the protective sheen of multiple intermeshed ironies, both individual and collective, we also know that our time is full of its own special conditions: special snares, risks, opportunities, promises.

3. So where should we look, in and through this particular here-and-now of ours, for a new ethic, a new and worthwhile value-set, a new delineation that fits our times and our predicament? The key to our lives and to our practice as poets, I believe, is in honouring and loving the universal in the particular and the particular in the universal.

4. Since the 1940s, a gradual, powerful, unstoppable, universalist tendency has been under way among poets. This tendency is everywhere apparent, all over the world, so much so that it's more or less taken for granted as an accepted, obvious feature of our

contemporary culture, wherever we live, from Burma to Britain, China to Chile, Macedonia to Mongolia.

5. In 1959, the Mexican poet and Nobel laureate Octavio Paz (1914–1988) – and my personal friend and mentor – wrote: "For the first time in our history, we are contemporaries of all humanity" (Paz 182; tr. slightly amended).

6. This remark presents a model of hope, compassion, tolerance, magnanimity and aspiration for the future, grounded in the Universal Declaration of Human Rights ratified by the United Nations General Assembly in 1948.

7. The universalist tendency in poetry today is founded on twin premises or beliefs, whether explicit or subliminal. The first is that all human beings, and hence the cultures of all peoples and nations – past, present and future – are all tributaries to the one great river. This is of course both an old view and a new one. Considering his own mortality, the seventeenth century English poet and Anglican priest John Donne (1572–1631) expressed this identical idea, though by means of a slightly different geographical metaphor:

> No man is an island, entire of itself; every man is a piece of the continent, a part of the main. If a clod be washed away by the sea, Europe is the less, as well as if any promontory were, as well as if a manor of thy friend's or of thine own were: any man's death diminishes me, because I am involved in mankind, and therefore never send to know for whom the bell tolls; it tolls for thee. (Donne 108-109)

Retrospectively, this statement by Donne is limited only by its Eurocentricity. Its dazzling dignity, depth and delicacy surpass that limitation. But what makes Paz's vision *new* – not only newer than Donne's but more relevant to our present, more pressing in its urgency, and more joyful in its implications, is the fact that it operates *explicitly* for everyone, not just within one religion, nation, ethnicity, time, place, etc., but incorporating all human beings, everywhere and everywhen, regardless of aspect, background, context, or any other factors of any kind.

Donne's statement is itself all-inclusive: Paz's makes it not only incontrovertible, but a basis for action.

8. The second premise, which underlies the first, is that differences among cultures, nations, languages, etc. at different times and places are as natural, necessary and inevitable as is the fact of diversity among biological species. What is more, implicit in this understanding is the recognition that diversities are *great gifts and treasures*. They are nothing short of *glories*.* It follows, then, that the idiosyncratic expressions and manifestations of all cultures are to be respected, honoured and loved – precisely *for* their uniquenesses.

9. And here, the ideas and practices of two more visionary English poets offer foundations for our necessary love and respect for diversity, for uniquenesses, for what *we* are given and for what others are given. The first of these is William Blake (1757–1827), who wrote repeatedly of "the minute particulars". These are interpreted by S. Foster Damon as "the outward expression in this world of the eternal individualities of all things" (Damon 280). For Blake, any universalist vision without love of these "minute particulars" is abhorrent: the vilest of vile prisons, a mechanistic abnegation of human freedom and Imagination, a hell.

10. The second poet is the Jesuit priest Gerard Manley Hopkins (1844–1889), whose study of the medieval philosopher and theologian Duns Scotus's notion of *haeceittas* or 'thisness' led him to celebrate what he called the 'instress' and 'inscape' of things (Hopkins 1966: 572; and 2013: 1039): their individual unique quality, their glory. This is identical to what, in the Jewish Kabbalistic tradition, is called the *Shekhinah* (see Scholem 1955: 454; and 1991: 326). Here is what Hopkins says as he looks at a glass of flowers: "Take a *few* primroses in a glass and the instress of – brilliancy, sort of starriness [...] – so simple a flower gives is remarkable" (Hopkins 1966: 206).

11. This understanding of the uniqueness, the instress, the beauty of flowers is central to any poetic vision: Compare Hopkins's remarks with these famous lines of Blake:

To see a World in a Grain of Sand
And a Heaven in a Wild Flower,
Hold Infinity in the palm of your hand
And Eternity in an hour.

When we are considering multiplicity in the context of a necessary tolerance and universalism, then I suggest that what's needed above all is *the feeling eye of the poet*, which combines awareness of what the ancient Greek philosophers called το έν και το πάν [*to en kai to pan*], 'the *one* and the *many*': that is, the majesty of indivisible and encompassing oneness and the glory and majesty of diversity.

12. So, if you want to appreciate diversity, and to respect the unique dignity and *thisness* of each separate being, and the achievements and glories of each separate tradition and each separate language, start by looking at flowers again, and do so with the eye of a poet.

REFERENCES

Blake, William. 1927. 'Auguries of Innocence'. In *Poetry and Prose of William Blake*. Keynes, Geoffrey (ed.). London: Nonesuch Press: 118.

Damon, S. Foster. 1973. *A Blake Dictionary*. London: Thames and Hudson.

Donne, John. 1959. *Devotions upon Emergent Occasions*. Ann Arbor, MI: University of Michigan Press.

Hopkins, Gerard Manley. 1966. *The Journals and Papers of Gerard Manley Hopkins*. House, Humphrey (ed.). Oxford: Oxford University Press.

————. 2013. *The Collected Works*, vols. 1 and 2: *Correspondence*. Thornton, R. K. R. and Phillips, Catherine (eds.) Oxford: Oxford University Press.

Paz, Octavio. 1967, *The Labyrinth of Solitude*. Kemp, Lysander (tr.). London: Allen Lane, the Penguin Press.

Scholem, Gershon. 1955. *Major Trends in Jewish Mysticism*. London: Thames and Hudson.

————. 1991. *On the Mystical Shape of the Godhead: Basic Concepts in the Kabbalah*. New York, NY: Schocken Books.

On Poetry and Exile

Twelve Propositions

1. Who is not in exile. We make and remake poems and songs, so that we may go home again. To this making there is no end.

2. Home is by definition where mine is shared with you and yours is with me. Making a poem or song is a transmission that is a giving and a receiving, a two-way reciprocity, even when you or I write or sing alone and into apparently prevailing silence(s). Receiving or making a song or poem itself enables you and/or me to feel, think and believe, even if only for an eyeblink: Why, this (here, now) *is* home.

3. History is exile from eternity. Who doesn't live in history. Poetry (song) inserts us momentarily into a corner or station of eternity. Or maybe (even) into eternity's core? At any rate, not merely into a self-forgetting or dream, but a re-membering that is a double waking.

4. When a poem sings inside you, aren't you at one with everything.

5. The poem says: The past hasn't yet even started, let alone happened, and the future came and went ages ago. The past is a seedling and the future, ashes.

6. On the ashes of the future the phoenix of this (here, now) cracks its eggshells and takes flight in flame. That sound in the grate? Its newborn ancestor-descendent in the act of being born – singing.

7. My dead father Alexander Israel Berengarten came to me in a dream and said: "I hear you're a poet. Are you a *good* poet?" I recognised this as a test and replied: "That's not for me to say. What I can say is, I'm a true poet." He smiled as if to say: "Pass."*

8. In another dream, William Blake met me in an underground chamber far beneath the streets of London, and opened two vents in a wall. The larger one was an entry to hell, the smaller

to paradise. He told me what I already half-knew, but I knew I had to hear it from him, there and then, not from anybody else or at any other time, to make it real: *To gain entry to the latter, first pass through the former.**

9. Poems and songs can't avoid being replete with ancestral voices. To open oneself and clarify oneself sufficiently to listen to them.

10. To listen to the ancestral voices and to love and respect them. But also to let our poems and songs question and test their bounds, before we too pass on. For *Alas! We lodge in the body for a hundred years and end in the twinkling of an eye.**

11. In making poetry and song, do we wake or dream we wake? If the latter, are poems and songs the best parts of this double-dream of waking?

12. A host/hostess that matter-of-factly holds open house anywhere and anywhen, the poem offers you perpetual hospitality.

On Poetry and Morning

Twelve Observations

1. Dispassionate morning greets me. I breathe into rain-sounds, sleep-filled, dream-billowed. My flat roof creaks, pitter-patters.

2. It holds above me. The world that bears me confirms it's in place.

3. But dreaming hasn't done with me, still has things to tell, pulls me back, clutching, withholding me from day.

4. Pen and notebook wait. Thanks to these attendants, the dream, already fading, writes its dim echoes out of me, then drifts away, turning to nothing.

5. This breath is key of keys. Being both mine and not, it joins me to the world. It binds us together.

6. Preceding even firstness, originary infinitive, prior to enunciation, subjectless and objectless, anterior to precedence, priority, numeration – here again, light, hello.

7. Is breath inpouring, the fifth person singular? Is breath exhaling, the seventh person plural?

8. I taste light and breath. I wash them through lips onto tongue. Round and round I curl them. I coil them and recoil them. On the alveolar ridge I cool them. On the velar roof I warm them. Over the glottis I gurgle them.

9. Breath coursing through me becomes inner light.

10. Limbs move and stretch. This animal gets up.

11. It doesn't matter to morning whether anybody or anything happens (to be) in it or not. But it's morning's nature to greet.

12. And this particular morning swells sonorous and deep, and very sweet and full, here-now, in Cambridge, England. How can I not reciprocate. Good morning, morning.

Notes

All online references were rechecked in May 2019. Asterisks in the above texts refer to asterisked notes below.

Title

I've coined the term 'imagem' with the meaning 'nexus, web, net, body, corpus, etc., of integrally associated ideas and images'. An *imagem* is composite, complex and polysemic. It also implies 'unit of imagery', comparable to the word *mythologem* ('unit of myth or mythology', or, as defined by the OED online, "fundamental theme or motif of myth or other discourse"). I think such a term is helpful in English because it fills a conceptual gap. Shortly after arriving at this term, together with its first, tentative definition, I discovered that it already exists in Portuguese, meaning, simply, *image*. See also p. 12, para. 11 above.

Epigraphs

1. William Wordsworth, *The Excursion: being a portion of The Recluse, a Poem*. 1814. London: Longman, Hurst, Rees, Orme & Brown. Online at: https://en.wikisource.org/wiki/The_Excursion
2. Iain McGilchrist, *The Master and his Emissary*. 2010. New Haven, CT: Yale University Press, 229.
3. Pierre Bourdieu, *Language and Symbolic Power*. 1992. Gino Raymond and Matthew Adamson (trs.). Cambridge: Polity Press, 41.

On Poetry and Sound: The Ontogenesis of Poetry, pp. 7-12

For Antonio Dominguez-Rey

Composed January 21-23, 2009; revised August 25, 2015.

I'm indebted to Antonio Dominguez Rey for exploring some of the ideas that found their way into this piece, as he drove me from Padron to Rianxo on the evening of November 29, 2008, at the end of the ninth international seminar on language(s), translation and poetics [*lingua(s), tradución e poética*], which was conducted in Spanish, Galician and English. He pointed out that some of these ideas derive from Ortega y Gasset.

* p. 7, para. 2, line 8: safety, security and surety – three concepts that combine in the German word *Sicherheit*.

On the Breath and the Cry, pp. 13-14

To honour Charles Olson (1910–1970) and Philip Lieberman; and for my grandchildren, Imogen Lightning, Alexander Lightning and Eli Burns. Composed, Cambridge, April 1, 2009 and April 2, 2019.

On Writing and Inner Speech, pp. 15-22
For Will Hill
Composed, Cambridge, November 11, 2014, June 19, 2015, August 25, 2015, and April-May 2019.

* p. 15, para. 1, ll. 3ff. Lev Vygotsky was a brilliant Russian-Jewish developmental psychologist who died of tuberculosis, aged 37, in 1934. Living and working in the Stalinist period, he had to couch both his theories and experimental conclusions in strict accordance not only with scientific methodology but also with Communist doctrine. Despite self-doubts and personal crises, it's an extraordinary achievement that he managed to do that, though it's very likely that the strain of conforming with Soviet orthodoxy was a factor in his deteriorating health and untimely death.

One of Vygotsky's major works, Мышление и речь [*Myshlenie i rech*] was published in Russia in 1934 but not translated into English until 1962. The Russian title is translatable into English in various ways: for example, *Thinking and Speaking, Thought and Speech, Thinking and the Word, Thought and Word, Thought and Language*, etc. Evidently, not one of these alone does full justice to the echoic resonance of the Russian. The title chosen for the 1962 English edition was *Thought and Language* (trs. Eugenia Hanfmann and Gertrude Walker, MIT Press, Cambridge, MA.). Since then, the book has had a powerful and increasingly pervasive influence on theories of children's conceptual and linguistic development. The edition I've used, and refer to here, was re-edited by Alex Kozulin (MIT Press, 2012).

One of the key notions in this book is that of "inner speech". In the course of an extensive critique of Piaget, according to Vygotsky the young child develops "egocentric" speech, based on the social speech s/he hears in the immediate environment, but with the difference that in egocentric speech the child is both speaker and listener, i.e. intends the speech for herself/himself, talks *to* herself/himself:

> If we compare the amount of what might be called egocentric speech of children and adults, we would have to admit that the "egocentric" speech of adults is much richer. From the point of view of functional psychology all silent thinking is nothing but "egocentric" speech. John B. Watson would have said that such speech serves individual rather than social adaptation. (Vygotsky 2012: 34)

In the same key passage, Vygotsky spells out that inner speech continues into adulthood:

The first feature uniting the inner speech of adults with the egocentric speech of children is its function as speech-for-oneself. (ibid. 34)

Vygotsky then clarifies that both egocentric speech and inner speech "would be incomprehensible to others because they omit to mention what is obvious to the speaker" and that "when egocentric speech disappears, it does not simply atrophy but 'goes underground,' i.e. turns into inner speech." Inner speech, then, is elliptical and cryptic; and what it does include suggests that it contains more than it 'says'. Later he argues that "egocentric speech as a separate linguistic form is the highly important genetic link in the transition from vocal to inner speech" (ibid. 37).

Vygotsky's theory, in my view, serves as the foundation for a powerful and radical rethinking of *writing* itself. As these 'Twelve Propositions' clarify, I believe writing results from the development and refinement of inner speech.

* p. 15. para 1, end. In addition to generating both oral speech and written script, preparatory inner speech is also integral to a vast range of entirely non-verbally-expressed actions and activities. See, for example, Hamlet's self-debate about moral qualms, irresolution and action: "Thus conscience does make cowards of us all; / And thus the native hue of resolution / Is sicklied o'er with the pale cast of thought [...] (*Hamlet*, Act III, Sc. 1, ll. 91-93). The 52nd hexagram of the *I Ching* also clarifies that 'action' includes non-action: silence, keeping still. See Richard Wilhelm and Cary F. Baynes (trs.). 1965 [1951]. *The I Ching, or Book of Changes*, Routledge and Kegan Paul: London: 200-203 and 652-656; and RB, 'Stilling', *Changing*, Shearsman Books, Bristol, 2017: 415-423.

* p. 15. para. 2, end. From the fifth verse of a much-translated poem, number 113 in Mandelstam's sequence *Tristia*, written in November 1920, and usually referred to as 'The Swallow'. These lines are bravely quoted by Vygotsky as the epigraph to the final chapter of *Thought and Language* (1934), as a telling indicator of his theory of 'inner speech' – bravely, because Mandelstam was already under Stalin's suspicion. See *Thought and Language* 2012: 223. Variant possible translations for Russian 'безплотная' ('bez-plotnaya') include *voiceless, unvoiced, unbodied, unembodied* and *intangible*.

ON UNIVERSALISM AND PARTICULARISM: pp. 23-26
For Chen Shangzhen
Composed, Cambridge, March 27-30, 2016.

* p. 25, para 8, l. 6. For more on "glory" and "glories", see RB, *Imagems 1*, Shearsman Books, Bristol, 2013: 14-22.

On Poetry and Exile, pp. 27-28
In memory of Sydney Bolt (1920–1992)
Composed, Cambridge, January 21-22, 2009; April 9, 2017; and April 2, 2019.

    * p. 27, para. 7. See also 'Ghost, revisiting' and 'Ghost, questioning', in RB, *Changing*, Shearsman Books, Bristol, 2017, section 61/5-6: 493 and 494.

    * p. 28, para. 8. See also 'Ghost, revisiting' in *Book With No Back Cover*, 'Sketches with Voice-Overs' 16, David Paul, London, 2004: 30-31.

    * p. 28, para 10, ll. 2-3. See A. R. Davis, *T'ao Yüan-ming, His Works and their Meaning*, 'Moved by Scholars Not Meeting with Good Fortune' (poem 56) vol. 1: 177. For the Chinese context, see vol. 2: 135: 《易寓形百年而瞬息已盡。》

On Poetry and Morning, pp. 29-30
In memory of Peter Mansfield (1942–2009)
Composed, Cambridge, April 4 and 5, 2009; April 21, 2009; April 9, 2017; April 3 and 10, 2019.

CPSIA information can be obtained
at www.ICGtesting.com
Printed in the USA
LVHW091451011219
639066LV00004B/686/P